WITHDRAWN

KARL MARX

KARL MARX

PHILOSOPHER & REVOLUTIONARY

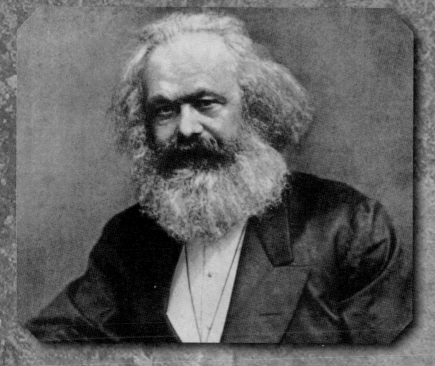

by David Cates

Content Consultant:
Marc Blecher, PhD, professor of politics and
East Asian studies, Department of Politics, Oberlin College

ABDO

CREDITS

Published by ABDO Publishing Company, 8000 West 78th Street, Edina, Minnesota 55439. Copyright © 2012 by Abdo Consulting Group, Inc. International copyrights reserved in all countries. No part of this book may be reproduced in any form without written permission from the publisher. The Essential Library™ is a trademark and logo of ABDO Publishing Company.

Printed in the United States of America,
North Mankato, Minnesota
062011
092011

♻ THIS BOOK CONTAINS AT LEAST 10% RECYCLED MATERIALS.

Editor: Holly Saari and Mari Kesselring
Copy Editor: Rebecca Rowell
Interior Design and Production: Kazuko Collins
Cover Design: Kazuko Collins

Library of Congress Cataloging-in-Publication Data
Cates, David, 1963-
    Karl Marx : philosopher & revolutionary / by David Cates.
        p. cm. -- (Essential lives)
    Includes bibliographical references.
    ISBN 978-1-61783-005-1
    1. Marx, Karl, 1818-1883--Juvenile literature. 2. Communists-
-Germany--Biography--Juvenile literature. 3. Philosophers--
Germany--Biography--Juvenile literature. I. Title.
    HX39.5.C38 2012
    335.4092--dc22
    [B]
                                                    2011007603

TABLE OF CONTENTS

Karl Marx was arrested in Brussels, Belgium, in 1848.

INSURRECTION AND ARREST

In early March 1848, a family in Brussels, Belgium, was hurriedly packing their belongings in preparation to flee the city. King Leopold II had signed an order forever expelling the family from the country. They had only 24 hours to settle their affairs, gather their belongings, and leave. In the midst of packing, a police commissioner and ten policemen burst into the family's home. The police ignored the official expulsion order and arrested the father for having no passport. The father was led away to prison. His name was Karl Marx, and he was not only father to his family; he also became the father of communism and one of the leading critical theorists of capitalism.

Revolutionary Ideas

Marx had been working hard as a journalist to spread his economic and social ideas, which relied heavily on revolution. Marx critiqued current social institutions such as governments and churches. He disliked capitalism—the system where industry is privately owned and operated for profit—and the group who profited from it, which Marx

An Exploitative King

Belgium's King Leopold II exemplified the type of ruler Marx sought to overthrow. Through trade, torture, and trickery, Leopold II controlled the African Congo. He did this in his own name, not in the name of Belgium. Leopold II sent Sir Henry Morton Stanley to get as much land in the Congo as was possible. When he met tribal chiefs, Stanley held an electric buzzer so they would receive a shock when he shook their hands. The Africans believed Stanley had magical power. Leopold II ruled the Africans brutally, using forced labor to harvest rubber and other natural resources, while he became rich from the profits.

called the bourgeoisie. Marx favored communism— the economic system where all property is publicly owned and people do not get goods through markets— to capitalism.

Not long before his arrest, Marx had received an advance of 6,000 francs, approximately $1,279, on his inheritance. He immediately donated most of the money— 5,000 francs, about $1,065—to help arm Belgian workers. He had been attending small meetings of workers, teaching them the art of insurrection, or

---

Revolutions in Europe

In 1848, almost all of Europe, including France, Prussia, Italy, and Poland, was afire with revolution. Alexis de Tocqueville, a historian of the time, said of this period, "Society was cut in two: those who had nothing united in common envy, and those who had anything united in common terror."[1] In other words, Tocqueville asserted that there were two different conflicting classes in Europe: the working poor, who had nothing, and the aristocracy, who had something and were often in positions of power as monarchs. There were uprisings of the poor against those in power. But the aristocrats were not terrified. Rather, they usually crushed the revolting poor, with casualties in the tens of thousands.

There was a third group that Tocqueville did not consider: the rising middle class, the group Marx called the bourgeoisie. While Marx predicted the rise of the workers over all other groups to establish an egalitarian society, the revolutions of 1848 saw the bourgeoisie and the workers uniting to petition for democratic rights. But fearing the threat of losing wealth in a true revolution, the bourgeoisie ultimately sided with royalty to reinstate deposed kings. The revolutions of 1848 resulted in measures that kept the wealth in the hands of those with power.

revolt. Marx hoped his material and ideological contributions would lead to a bloody overthrow of the Belgian bourgeoisie.

Marx was not the only person attempting to change society at this time. Revolutionaries across Europe, from France to Poland, were overthrowing their countries' governments. The Belgian government had no intention of falling. It employed spies to keep track of the activities and locations of revolutionaries within their country, and Marx was at the top of their list.

ARREST AND RELEASE

Marx was captured by the government he had worked to overthrow. He expected little mercy from the police, since he had heard the stories of brutal beatings that revolutionaries suffered while in police custody. And the clock was ticking. If he remained in Belgium

Changing Views

Ironically, at a New Year's Eve party just months before his arrest and expulsion from Belgium, Marx was full of praise for the country. He proposed a toast to Belgium, expressing his wholehearted appreciation for a country where a liberal constitution would allow for freedom of discussion and assembly. After his arrest, Marx denounced the "unprecedented brutality" and "reactionary fury" of a Belgium he once idealized.[2]

after the 24-hour deadline, Marx could be executed for the contributions he had made to arm the workers.

Soon after his arrest, Marx's wife, Jenny, was arrested. The next morning, the Marxes appeared before a court magistrate, who commented on the unfairness of their arrest and incarceration. He then dismissed the charges against them, and the Marxes were free to leave jail and the country.

Paris Bound

Although the 24-hour deadline had passed, the Marxes were allowed to return home. The couple retrieved their children and quickly packed the possessions they could take with them, leaving many of their cherished belongings behind. The family was taken by police escort to the railway station, where they boarded a train bound for Paris, France.

The Belgian government could not know they had just let slip a man whose ideas would inspire the toppling of many governments and facilitate the rise of some of the most powerful political regimes in modern history. ⌐

The Marxes escaped to Paris, France.

Karl was born in this house in Trier, Prussia.

CHILDHOOD AND SCHOOL DAYS

Karl Heinrich Marx was born on May 5, 1818, in the city of Trier, Prussia, one of present-day Germany's oldest cities. Unlike other German cities at the time, nineteenth-century Trier was a place where different philosophies about society and religion were openly discussed. Karl was raised in a town and family that valued free inquiry.

Karl was born to an esteemed Jewish family with generations of rabbis on his mother's and his father's sides. Despite the family tradition, Heinrich, Karl's father, was little influenced by Judaism. He was a lawyer and held an important position in city government. Little is known about Marx's mother, Henrietta. She was said to be a devoted wife and housekeeper and described as "stubborn" at times.[1]

Some people in Trier had anti-Semitic attitudes. In 1817, Heinrich had been warned that he would be fired from his job if he remained Jewish. Heinrich converted to Protestantism to keep his position. In 1824, the seven Marx children were baptized as Lutherans. Karl's mother was baptized shortly thereafter.

GROWING UP IN THE ENLIGHTENMENT

Karl grew up in a time historians call the Enlightenment, which was at its height during the eighteenth and

Karl's Motivation

Karl got his energy for his role as champion of the worker from the revolutions of his day, not from his own direct experience. He was born into a financially comfortable, respectable family and was privileged to receive a fine education. He never experienced the struggles of the workers first hand. In fact, he was more often than not unemployed, depending on the generosity of others to provide for him.

nineteenth centuries. As the power of the aristocracy was challenged, scholarly men—and a few women—became more influential than royalty or religion. Among other things, the Enlightenment addressed the value of science and the role and rights of the individual, including ownership of private property.

The Roman Catholic Church was a powerful force before this time. Those who challenged its doctrines or made scientific discoveries that opposed church beliefs could be labeled heretics and tortured or killed. The Enlightenment saw a decline in the power of the church and an intellectual challenge to church doctrine. Many debated the relevance of the church, and philosophers put human interests on an equal plane with the spiritual. Some people even demanded the end of all religions, espousing a doctrine of atheism. Heinrich was influenced by these thinkers, and so was Karl—he would come to believe religion

Religion Is Oppressive

Karl believed several aspects of society kept the working class unaware of being at the mercy of the bourgeoisie. He thought religion provided false comfort and hope to the working class, and hid the exploitation they met at the hands of the bourgeoisie. In 1843, in *The Critique of Hegel's Philosophy of Right*, he wrote, "Religion is the sigh of the oppressed creature, the heart of a heartless world, and the soul of soulless conditions. It is the opium of the people."[2]

was an institution that distracted the poor from understanding the power relations in society.

EDUCATION

Karl was probably educated at home until the age of 12, when he entered the local high school, Trier Gymnasium. Students liked Karl because he was always ready to pull a prank, but they feared him as well because Karl could write biting poems about his enemies. Schoolmates described Karl as haughty and arrogant, qualities that would define him throughout his life.

Karl's overall performance in high school was average. His exit exams show only fair results. Surprisingly, he scored lowest in history, a subject about which he would spend much of his adult life theorizing.

In 1835, Karl began attending the University of Bonn. Heinrich chose the school for his son. Rather than having a reputation for high intellectual standards, the university had something of a country club atmosphere. Karl joined in readily, becoming president of the Trier Tavern Club, an organization that focused mainly on drinking alcohol. The behavior was not productive, and Karl was ultimately arrested for public drunkenness and even wounded in a duel.

While at the university, Karl fancied himself a poet. When he was not drinking or brawling, he wrote verse with others in a poetry club he created. At one point, Karl asked his father for money to publish his poems. Heinrich refused. Shortly after this request, Heinrich decided that Bonn was not the best place for his son. He enrolled Karl in the much more rigorous University of Berlin for his son's sophomore year.

During the summer of 1836, before beginning his studies in Berlin, Karl returned home to Trier, where he began courting childhood friend Jenny von Westphalen. Four years older than Karl, she was known as a true beauty in their hometown. She inspired more verse from the love-struck poet. At the University of Berlin, Karl was more studious. He focused on law and philosophy. And his love for writing continued. He found time to write two novels—one comedy and one tragedy—and several collections of poetry for Jenny.

In 1838, during his second year at the University of Berlin, Karl received devastating news. His father had died. Karl was distraught, which affected his work. His writings dwindled and then stopped completely. He seemed directionless, spending much of his time in coffeehouses engaging in philosophical discussions. Karl also spent large sums of his family's money. He lived beyond his means and accrued debt. These money troubles would follow him throughout his life.

A GROWING PERSONAL PHILOSOPHY

Over the course of his studies in Berlin, Marx began exploring philosophical ideas that would shape the work he would do. At this point, his philosophy had three key components: atheism, the philosophical system proposed by Georg Wilhelm Friedrich Hegel, and the detrimental impact of the Industrial Revolution on the working class.

Marx was a committed atheist. He saw organized religion more as

Europe and the German Question

In the nineteenth century, Europe was a collection of monarchies, empires, and smaller states. The larger governments in Europe were the monarchy of England and the three empires of France, Prussia, and Austria. There was no country called Germany, but there was the German Confederation, a loose association of 39 German states, including the empires of Prussia and Austria.

Throughout the nineteenth century, the issue of whether or not Germany would become a nation-state unto itself was debated by the states of the confederation. This came to be called the German Question. Power struggles between the two greatest powers in the confederation, Prussia and Austria, would prevent any real unification. But in 1871, the German states were unified and the single nation-state Germany emerged.

an institution that enabled the powerful to control the weak than a path toward personal salvation. His childhood may have contributed to his disbelief in a higher power. Although his father converted to Christianity, Marx thought little of organized religion. Instead, he believed in the Enlightenment view that humankind's ability to reason, not the will of God, was the most important aspect of life. Also, while in college, Marx studied the writings of the contemporary philosopher Voltaire, who had sworn to eradicate religion.

The second component of Marx's personal philosophy was borrowed from the philosophy of Hegel, an influential philosopher of the day. A main point of Hegel's thought that greatly influenced Marx was that history progresses toward an end where all people are ultimately free. Marx found great value in Hegel's idea that history is created by conflicting ideas that result in a new idea. Hegel also believed that faith played an integral, beneficial part in moving societies toward this freedom. Marx disagreed and veered from Hegel's proposition that Christianity and the relationship between people and God lead to the highest truths. Marx may have criticized the spiritual element of Hegelian thought, but the part of

Hegel's philosophy that predicted a future of freedom dominated Marx's thinking. He simply thought the road to the future would pass through revolution, not religion.

The final aspect of Marx's philosophy stemmed from the Industrial Revolution and its resulting exploitation of the working class, a group Marx called the proletariat. The Industrial Revolution was the shift from an agricultural economy to an economy based on industry. It began in England in the late eighteenth century and spread throughout Europe. The Industrial Revolution led to many people

Hegel's Thought

A key element to Hegel's philosophy was his dialectics. Dialectics are a method of looking at reality as a product of the interplay of parts. Hegel proposed that when there is a thesis, or idea, there will also be an antithesis, or contrasting idea. These two ideas are then brought together to form a synthesis, or new idea, that combines elements of the thesis and antithesis. The new idea is considered a thesis, and the process starts over again. For example, the concept of a day is composed of the opposite parts of day and night. Dialectics have influenced some of the great thinkers of human history.

Hegel also believed in a dialectical system of the civil society and the state, or government. The state was the ultimate area where Hegel saw dialectics at work. In this dynamic, the state would eventually arise to serve the needs and ultimate good of its citizens. According to Hegel, history was moving in the direction of developing such a state. This component of Hegel's philosophy was of particular interest to Marx, who was curious about the evolution of the state.

Farming Advancements

Until the late eighteenth century, humans farmed using animal power and manual methods. Advances in farming tools and equipment beginning in the late eighteenth century made farming much more efficient, requiring fewer workers to harvest larger crops. For example, in 1830, it took approximately 300 hours of labor to produce 100 bushels of wheat using hand tools. By 1890, it took approximately 50 hours of labor to produce the same amount of wheat. This increase in production fed the growing European population and allowed unneeded laborers to migrate to the cities where they became factory workers.

moving from rural areas to cities to work in factories. As factories opened, a powerful new class emerged: the bourgeoisie, or middle-class factory owners.

Factory workers toiled for long hours and for low wages. Working conditions were often dangerous because of crowded production floors and unsafe equipment. Child labor was common. Workers struggled to afford housing and had to live in crowded, impoverished areas rife with unsanitary conditions and crime.

Marx considered the capitalistic system that led to the exploitation of workers a crime and the bourgeoisie who profited from this system as criminals. In 1841, Marx earned his doctorate degree at the University of Berlin, and he would soon dedicate himself to inspiring the workers to rise up and crush the bourgeoisie with violence and finality.

Georg Wilhelm Friedrich Hegel's philosophical system intrigued Marx.

Marx wrote for the Rheinische Zeitung.

A Journalist

After college, Marx was unsure of his direction in life. He had a degree in law, but he did not want to be a lawyer in his homeland of Prussia because he considered the government oppressive and in conflict with his own ideas.

In 1842, Marx moved to the industrial center of Cologne, Prussia, where he came upon an opportunity that would lead to a lifelong career. Through one of his connections, Marx was asked to write for the *Rheinische Zeitung*, a newspaper that catered to the liberal aristocracy of Cologne. The newspaper caught the unfavorable attention of the Prussian government, which was quick to censor it. But this did not dissuade the young journalist.

Kind Words for Marx

Moses Hess, friend of Marx's, once described him in glowing terms: "He is a phenomenon who made a tremendous impression on me in spite of the strong similarity of our fields. In short you can prepare yourself to meet the greatest—perhaps the only genuine—philosopher of the current generation. When he makes a public appearance whether in writing or in the lecture hall, he will attract the attention of all Germany."[1]

EARLY IDEAS ON COMMUNISM

Through this newspaper, Marx began to express his political and social ideas. He wrote articles about freedom of the press and the rights of the working class and the poor, but his ideas were not as radical as they would later become.

A young man around 24 years old at this time, Marx was idealistic, but he rejected the claims of socialism and communism that he began encountering. Socialism is an economic system that advocates for public ownership of property.

Marx, center, became editor of the Rheinische Zeitung.

Communism goes further in advocating the end of
the very idea of ownership itself. Just as no one owns
the air or the oceans, Communists look to an ideal
society in which everything would be freely accessible
to everyone. Communism promotes the equality
and financial security of all people. At the time, its
proponents often took up the fight of the mistreated
working class, which led to conflict, sometimes
violent, between the social classes. At this time in
his life, Marx believed communism was bound to
fail and any sort of class struggle would be resolved
peacefully.

Karl Marx

Marx the Editor

In 1842, the editor of the *Rheinische Zeitung* was dismissed, and Marx took over the position. He used his new position to command complete control of the newspaper. Marx quickly targeted two colleagues with whom he had begun writing at the paper. He believed they were trying to smuggle Communist ideas into their articles. Marx would not tolerate such behavior and fired them.

Marx was editor for five months. In that time, he wrote articles challenging the rights of the rich and exposing the methods by which they exploited the peasantry. Though not yet a Communist, he was an adamant atheist, which affected his writing. Marx came into possession of a government document that had been smuggled from Berlin. The document revealed that stricter regulations on divorce were being planned. Marx interpreted this as

Critic of Communism

In the editorial policy for the *Rheinische Zeitung*, Marx stated that the newspaper would remain a critic of communism: "The *Rheinische Zeitung*, which does not even admit that communist ideas in their present form possess even *theoretical reality*, and therefore can still less desire their *practical realisation*, or even consider it possible, will subject these ideas to thoroughgoing criticism."[2] It would be only a matter of years before Marx would assert that Communist ideas not only possessed theoretical reality, but that Communist ideas were the only reality.

religious institutions influencing the government on matters that should be left to the people. He published the document and a biting editorial condemning religion and the government.

However, as a result of Marx's criticism of the government's lack of authority, the Prussian minister of the interior ordered the *Rheinische Zeitung* shut down and Marx dismissed. Marx tried to postpone his firing but soon found himself unemployed. Yet, he was thankful to no longer worry about government censorship.

Shortly after leaving the *Rheinische Zeitung*, and after seven years of engagement, Marx and Jenny von

Jenny Marx

Marx's wife, Jenny, was from an influential family in Trier, Marx's hometown. She was the daughter of Baron von Westphalen. Jenny broke off her engagement with an officer and became engaged to Marx in 1836. The engagement was kept secret from Jenny's family for almost a year. While Marx was away at college, Jenny stayed in Trier.

Jenny's life with Marx was difficult. Marx was a professional revolutionary, moving from city to city where he felt he could have the most impact. Along the way, he earned little. Jenny followed along, making ends meet as best she could, at times having to face the same legal risks as Marx.

Jenny also had to provide for her growing family. The Marxes had six children. Two died within a year of birth, and another died at the age of nine. The family often lived in dire poverty, with little to eat and creditors at the door ready to take the few things the family owned. There were times when Jenny had to beg her family or friends for money so the family could have food and shelter.

Westphalen married. Frustrated with the censorship and oppression he felt in Prussia, Marx longed to leave his homeland. In 1843, he and his new bride headed for the revolutionary hotbed of Paris, France. After adjusting to the new city, Marx became coeditor of the *German-French Yearbooks*, a magazine that was first banned in Prussia and had moved to Paris. Hoping to avoid the attention censors gave to magazines, the *German-French Yearbooks* were sold in book form.

While at the *German-French Yearbooks*, Marx began to develop ideas that would become central to his changing views on communism. For example, in the *German-French Yearbooks*, Marx advocated, dialectically, the violent overthrow of capitalism by the proletariat, a task that would be made easier by the likelihood of capitalism toppling from its own internal problems.

Free from Censorship

In a letter to his friend Arnold Ruge, Marx expressed his relief to be free from under the control of the Prussian censors: "It's a bad thing to perform menial duties even for the sake of freedom; to fight with pinpricks, instead of clubs. I have become tired of hypocrisy, stupidity, gross arbitrariness, and of our bowing and scraping, dodging, and hair-splitting over words. Consequently, the government has given me back my freedom."[3]

The intellectual and literary circles in France barely noticed the *German-French Yearbooks*. They were, however, read by the Prussian minister to France, who demanded that copies of the *German-French Yearbooks* intended for Prussia be destroyed. In addition, the Prussian government turned its attention to Marx. He was to be arrested on sight should he return to Prussia.

Marx married Jenny von Westphalen in 1843.

Friedrich Engels circa 1850

COMMITTING TO
COMMUNISM

While in France, Marx began what would
become a lifelong relationship with
Friedrich Engels. Marx had met Engels once before,
and Engels had written some articles for the *Rheinische
Zeitung*. But in Paris, Marx and Engels became fast

friends and coconspirators in the revolution they increasingly saw as inevitable.

FRIEND, PARTNER, FINANCER

In September 1844, Engels began to write with Marx. Over the course of their 39-year relationship, the two coauthored many works. Sometimes, Engels worked as editor on Marx's pieces; sometimes, he wrote with Marx. Some works attributed to Marx have so many contributions by Engels that it is difficult to discern who the true author is.

Engels was not only a friend and a partner, but many times he supported Marx financially. Having come from a wealthy bourgeois family, Engels knew the value of money and how to manage it, unlike Marx, who seemed incapable of keeping money in his pocket. In their relationship, Marx would beg and cajole Engels without hesitation.

Miserable Working Conditions

Though Engels benefited directly from family ownership of factories, in 1844, he published *The Condition of the Working Class in England*, a book exposing the terrible working and living conditions of factory workers there. Engels wrote, "The reasons for this state of affairs are perfectly clear. First and foremost, factory work is largely responsible. Work in low rooms where people breathe more coal fumes and dust than oxygen—and in the majority of cases beginning already at the age of six—is bound to deprive them of all strength and joy in life."[1]

Engels would become one of the primary benefactors for Marx.

Writings and Criticisms

Marx wrote his first book, *Economic and Philosophic Manuscripts*, in 1844, although it would not be published until 1932. The book is essentially a brutal critique of contemporary ideas about socialism. While the book further affirms Marx's belief that capitalism is bound to fail, it also displays that Marx was not one to be opposed. The book is full of searing criticisms of his contemporaries' ideas.

This willingness to cut his peers to pieces was a well-known trait. Marx would not tolerate challenges to or criticisms of his ideas. Any disagreement with or critique of his work would lead Marx to venomous verbal and print retaliations. Marx was not only willing to attack on ideological and personal levels. He was also interested only in people who could further his cause. He could turn his back on a relationship as soon as he decided it was not useful. For example, in one publication Marx describes one rival as a "rowdy, loudmouth and extremely confused little manikin whose life-motto [is]: 'I would rather be an impudent windbag than nothing at all.'"[2] He describes another as having a "leathery appearance" with a "stupid expression," and yet another he declares has a "ferret-face."[3]

Toward Communism

As 1844 drew to a close, Marx had few prospects for work. He also had a police escort out of France. He had written a few articles for *Vorwarts!*, a German newspaper, that later praised the assassination attempt on King Friedrich Wilhelm IV of Prussia. Under pressure from the Prussian government, the French government expelled all of the nonnationals who wrote for the

The Bully

Marx was known for his bullying tactics. A friend commented that he did not use a pencil, but a Roman stylus, an instrument used to write as well as to stab. "The style," his friend said, "is the dagger used for a well-aimed thrust at the heart."[4] Using the stylus was symbolic of Marx's threatening nature and showed one of his methods of intimidation. Another friend said that Marx wanted to annihilate those who did not support his ideas without question. He described Marx as one who wanted to "break windowpanes with cannon."[5] In other words, Marx used big weapons even on small targets.

Marx spared no one when it came to criticism, and often those who thought themselves in Marx's favor would find themselves at the mercy of his sharp tongue. There were times when Marx's supporters would suggest "that a lion should not waste his time fighting with dung-beetles," that he was far too important to waste his time bickering with those beneath him.[6] He once responded, "Our task must be unsparing criticism, directed even more against our self-styled friends than against our declared enemies."[7]

paper. Marx was given four weeks to get his affairs in order and leave the country.

From France, Marx, along with Engels, moved to Brussels, Belgium, in 1845. After this move, Marx decided to renounce his Prussian citizenship. The Prussian government was happy to oblige. Being a man without a country was agreeable to Marx.

Though Marx was doubtful about communism in the beginning of his career, he now had full confidence in it. After settling in Brussels, Marx founded the Communist Party. At the time, there was little difference in the ideas of the Communists and the Socialists. But there was already a Socialist Party in France. Marx was not one to join in with the ideas of others and called his organization the Communist Party, so there could be no mistaking his group for another. Far from a group of revolutionary

Violence Is Necessary

Marx believed that, over time, the politics, social institutions, and values of an older society change and lead to a new society. Marx saw this as a gradual process leading to a dramatic conclusion in a revolution. He explained, "Violence is the midwife of every old society pregnant with a new one."[8] The old society metaphorically gives birth to the new society. Just as birth is a painful process facilitated by a midwife, Marx believed that it was violence that would bring the new society from the old one.

proletarians, Marx's Communist Party comprised approximately 20 middle-class intellectuals, most of whom were German.

Marx had his work cut out for him, but certain things happening in Europe made it more likely that the working class would embrace his ideas. Politically, the 1840s was a decade of upheaval. People were calling for more rights and freedoms—in short, a more democratic government. They did not want to be lorded over by a ruler of an empire. From 1846 to 1847, crop failures added to the dissatisfaction of Europeans. And with the rise of factories, an increased working class was having more influence on the development of capitalism.

Marx and Engels believed it was their duty to lead the growing and dissatisfied masses of the proletariat. They also believed it was their duty to eliminate those who would deceive the workers—mainly those who disagreed with Marx's thoughts and ideas. Marx and Engels began a systematic attack on those they felt opposed the true doctrine of Marx. Marx and Engels defeated some rivals in the party, but they were so insulting to their opponents that they alienated many who could possibly have spread and advocated for their philosophies.

*Marx, right, and Engels would work together on many
publications throughout their lives.*

Capitalism

Political changes were happening throughout the
world during the nineteenth century. Enlightenment
thinkers proposed a variety of different political
orders that challenged the feudal system. New
economic systems touted change. Proposed forms of
socialism promised an equal share of property for
everyone. Another economic system that arose was

capitalism. Capitalism is a system where the means of production, machines and factories, are privately owned, and the owners make a profit by selling what they make for more than what it costs to produce. Laissez-faire, or "hands off," capitalism is a form of capitalism where the ruling authority or government does not regulate capitalist production of goods.

Capitalism was the true target of all of Marx's theories. Since profits were the main goal of capitalism, he saw this system as inherently exploitative of the worker. The cheaper a product was to make, the more profit the owner would earn. As the Industrial Revolution continued, capitalist business practices increased. Marx believed business owners intentionally kept workers' wages low to keep production costs down. He thought those who owned the means of production were becoming rich on the blood and sweat of the common worker, who would receive less and less for more labor. Marx saw this as a terrible form of exploitation.

He decided his ideas would lead to the violent overthrow of the capitalist system and the rise of the proletariat. Marx imagined that the rise of the proletariat would be slow at first. It would destroy machinery and set fire to some factories.

As production increased, so would the masses of proletariat. Finally, when the number of proletarians reached a vast majority, they would move to destroy the bourgeoisie, annihilating them completely. The proletariat would create a peaceful world where no worker would want for anything.

Marx's economic and political philosophies had become well articulated, but they were still relatively unknown. He would soon have the opportunity to explain them to others in a short pamphlet that would become one of the most influential documents in history.

With the increase of factories, Marx was concerned
about the rights of workers.

Marx, with the help of Engels, wrote the Communist Manifesto.

A Famous Text

While economic changes were taking place that helped spread Marx's ideas, the political changes in Europe were not going the way Marx wanted. People were not moving toward the Communist society Marx foresaw.

Instead, Europeans were petitioning and rebelling for democratic change. Marx saw democracy as ultimately empowering the bourgeoisie by providing the proletariat with false hope of equality while distracting them from the ultimate goal: a world where there is no more want because there is no more private ownership.

One group, however, shared Marx's vision of the future. The League of the Just, a loose-knit association of German workers, believed in the imminent and violent overthrow of the bourgeoisie by the proletariat. Members thought the revolution was coming soon and that Marx was the one to unify and lead them through that revolution.

Marx Commissioned

In November 1847, the League of the Just met Marx in London, England, to commission him to write their party policy and aims. The League of the Just had spread across Europe, and the organization wanted a platform that would unify member groups in a common direction.

Marx and Engels began working on the pamphlet that month. As was his habit at times, Marx was slow to write. The league threatened to take legal action if he did not produce the piece, but he finally finished crafting it. The pamphlet, known as the *Communist Manifesto*, was first printed in German in February 1848 and later in French just before the French Revolution in June of the same year. With the translation of the *Communist Manifesto* to English two years later, the publication was accessible to almost everyone in Europe and the United States.

OVERVIEW OF THE *COMMUNIST MANIFESTO*

The actual title of the *Communist Manifesto* is the *Manifesto of the Communist Party*. The words *Communist Party* are used in the title to create an impression that Communists in Europe comprise a large, unified body—the Communist Party. Actually, there were a number of different Communist groups across Europe, but they were so loosely organized that it was a stretch to refer to them as a single party.

The style of the *Communist Manifesto* is similar to the style of a drama. It introduces heroes and villains and the ultimate conflict that results in the heroes vanquishing the villains forever. The eventual and rightful heroes of class struggle are the masses of proletarians that capitalism has produced. Marx casts the bourgeoisie as the ultimate enemy and exploiter of the proletariat. The end, of course, is that the proletarians rise and violently annihilate the bourgeoisie. Finally, the proletariat creates a society where all are content and there is no exploitation.

SECTION ONE

The *Communist Manifesto* has four sections. Section one charts the rise of the bourgeoisie from feudalism. Here, Marx claimed that as the bourgeoisie came into power, they turned skilled craftspeople into simple laborers. People who took pride—even pleasure—in working to produce

Fight for the League's Manifesto

As with many of Marx's works, the days leading up to the creation of the *Communist Manifesto* were fraught with intrigue. At the time, others in the League of the Just were working on documents of their own. It was imperative to Marx and Engels that they have control over the document that would proclaim the league's Communist agenda. Member Moses Hess had begun working on a draft of his own. At a meeting, Engels "ridiculed this document, line by line," so much so that the members threw it out and asked Engels to draft one of his own.[1] Engels wrote to Marx of his victory:

Completely unopposed, I got them to entrust me with the task of drafting a new [document] which will be discussed next Friday by the district and will be sent to London behind the backs of the communities. Naturally not a soul must know about this, otherwise we shall all be unseated.[2]

Engels had manipulated the league, turning it against one member and assuring that Engels's draft would be sent to the league's headquarters in London without review by the other league chapters. Later, Marx would take Engels's draft and turn it into the *Communist Manifesto*.

First Draft

Engels wrote a first draft of what would become the *Communist Manifesto* in the form of a catechism, a set form of questions and answers meant to inform. For example:

"Question 1: Are you a Communist?

Answer: Yes.

Question 2: What is the aim of the Communists?

Answer: To organize society in such a way that every member of it can develop and use all his capabilities and powers in complete freedom and without thereby infringing the basic conditions of this society.

Question 3: How do you wish to achieve this aim?

Answer: By the elimi-nation of private property and its replacement by community of property."[3]

Engels's draft contained more than 20 questions and their corresponding answers. Marx felt the piece should state Communist beliefs outright, which resulted in a more straightforward structure.

a quality product are made to understand only small parts of the production process and are put to work solely to make money.

Proceeding dialectically, Marx praised the achievements of the bourgeoisie. He stated that the bourgeoisie demonstrated the great creativity of society, greater by far than the accomplishments of the Egyptians, the Romans, and the earlier Europeans. But due to greed, the bourgeoisie took advantage of the proletariat by making its members work in the factories for declining wages, which resulted in increasing profit for the bourgeoisie.

Marx asserted that the bourgeoisie are guilty of four main crimes against society. The first crime, he argued, was that capitalists have destroyed local business by spreading industry across the world. Goods are no longer produced locally but in many different locations worldwide, so local industries are no longer able to keep up with competition and fail. Nationalism disappears because the bourgeoisie are not bound to a country; their factories are placed wherever in the world they can reap the most profit. Marx believed the spread of once-local industry throughout the world resembles the way a disease infects and destroys its host. He was the first modern critic of globalization, which he foresaw more than a century before it became a household word.

The second crime was mass production of goods creating a global culture. As cheaper goods flood into foreign countries, they are purchased and become part of the culture. In this way, bourgeois culture infiltrates the foreign culture. The foreigners become bourgeois themselves, which helps spread capitalism. The third crime was the impoverishment of the rural areas. As industry boomed, the population was drawn from rural areas to the cities. The urban population exploded, and wealth became centered in a few industrial cities.

The fourth and final crime was that the bourgeoisie exploit nature just as they do workers. Again, more than a century before the modern environmental movement, Marx argued that capitalists take what they need from the land, leaving a ravished landscape in their wake.

Marx believed these four crimes caused far-reaching consequences that the bourgeoisie could not prevent. He stated that while the bourgeoisie exploited humans and nature, their system created the proletarian class, which was already rising up against them.

Marx also pointed out the cycles of capitalism. In an attempt to increase profit, production is increased. In order to make more goods and a higher profit, the proletariat is forced to work longer hours for less money. This continues until so much is produced that profit can go no higher and there are no wages for the proletariat. Without wages, no one has money to buy products. The bourgeoisie searches for and finds new markets, and the cycle starts again. At the end of capitalism, there are no new markets and the system collapses completely.

During these cycles, the masses that make up the proletariat are increasing. More production means more factories, which require more workers. These masses of workers are concentrated in the cities because that is where the factories are located. When the bourgeois system fails, the proletariat stands ready to sweep in and destroy the last remnants of capitalism.

Section Two

Section two of the *Communist Manifesto* examines the relationship of communism to the proletariat. Private ownership of property is abolished and the wealth of the bourgeoisie is shared equally among the proletariat. According to Marx, "The theory of the communists may be summed up in the single sentence: Abolition of private property."[4]

Wage labor is abolished, having been a way for the bourgeoisie to make the proletariat work to merely survive and increase bourgeois profit. Marx proposed the end of the bourgeois family unit, which he claimed is based on profit and not love. He continued on to suggest the abolition of nations. Since workers are equal, there is no reason for hostilities among nations.

A Call to Arms

The last paragraph of the *Communist Manifesto* was an incendiary call to arms, or rallying cry: "Communists scorn to hide their views and aims. They openly declare that their purposes can only be achieved by the forcible overthrow of the entire existing social order. Let the ruling classes tremble at a communist revolution. Proletarians have nothing to lose but their chains. They have a world to win. Workingmen of all countries, unite!"[5]

Marx hoped the Communist Manifesto *would help spread revolutions among workers.*

Marx followed this with a list of ten reforms, including a push for public education for all and the reclamation of land by the government. None of these ideas were new at the time. Some had been proposed and enacted by the very leaders Marx sought to overthrow. The ideas did not include the appropriation of capitalist property.

The power of the *Communist Manifesto* comes not from the novelty of its ideas but by the way the ideas were brought together by Marx. In fact, none of the ideas contained within the *Communist Manifesto* were original to Marx. The most recognizable statements were authored by others: "The proletarians have nothing to lose but their chains" was written by the French philosopher Jean-Paul Marat; "the dictatorship of the proletariat" was coined by the French revolutionary Auguste Blanqui; and the rally cry of the proletariat, "Workingmen of all countries, unite!" was published four months before the *Communist Manifesto* was released.[6]

Sections Three and Four

The pamphlet is rounded out by two final sections. Section three criticizes different theories of socialism. Section four examines the relationship of communist ideas to other political systems. Sections three and four are not as relevant today as they were in Marx's time, when revolutions were breaking out across Europe. The first two sections, which focus on capitalism rather than communism, comprise the most influential parts of the document.

INFLUENCE OF THE *COMMUNIST MANIFESTO*

The *Communist Manifesto* would become one of
the most important and influential documents
in history, but it was little known during Marx's
lifetime. By the time it was printed, the revolutions
of 1848 were already in motion. The *Communist
Manifesto* did not spark those revolutions, which
Marx believed grew out of economic and political
conditions more than ideas in books. But Marx
thought its ideas, based on those conditions, would
help spread revolution. ⌐

Marx wrote much of the Communist Manifesto in a café once located in this Brussels building.

The February Revolution took place in Paris, France, in 1848.

EDITOR AGAIN

*I*n the weeks before Marx returned to Paris in 1848, after being exiled from Belgium by King Leopold II, the flames of the February Revolution had swept through the streets. Marx stepped off the train in Paris, ready to be welcomed by the revolutionary French government and to take up its cause, but he saw only the remnants of struggle. Walking through the streets of Paris, he saw blackened and burned-out buildings, broken windows, and the remains of barricades, but no active conflict.

Revolution only flashed and then smoldered in small groups across Europe. The government officials that had been challenged fled, conceded to the revolutionaries, or, in many cases, quashed the rebellions outright. Ultimately, it was not the few revolutionaries that came to power. The French elected moderate democrats to represent them. These representatives would address better working conditions and political rights for French citizens.

Marx was concerned that the populace seemed to be more intent on democratic ideals than Communist ones. He saw this as

The February Revolution

On February 22, 1848, French radical leaders held a banquet to protest for the right of universal suffrage—the right for all to vote. At the time, only those who owned a certain amount of land could vote. The French government banned the demonstration, but supporters gathered anyway. Fighting broke out. On February 23, the revolt reached its peak. Shots were fired by the French military, but many soldiers put down their guns and joined the demonstrators. The next day, what came to be known as the February Revolution ended with the abdication of the king, Louis-Philippe. The February Revolution sparked uprisings throughout Europe.

an incomplete struggle: the workers had begun to
change the status quo, but they had not gone far
enough to completely overthrow the political and
economic structures. He longed to see the fight
followed through to what he saw as the end—the
rise of the working class, where no one would be
dominated by someone more powerful. He believed
a violent overthrow was necessary, but not the type
he saw happening in this period. He did not see a
democratic government as the answer.

The members of larger Communist groups,
where Marx had some sway, either split into smaller
groups led by individuals with their own takes on
communism, or left the cause all together. Marx felt
his influence slipping. In an attempt to rouse the
revolutionary spirit in his homeland of Prussia, he
and other Communist leaders wrote *Demands of the
Communist Party in Germany*.

Demands of the Communist Party in Germany was printed
on a leaflet. The plan was to send hundreds of
German Communist refugees back to Prussia to
secretly distribute the document. The goal was to
incite a revolt. Only a few of the most dedicated
returned to Prussia with the document, and it did
little to influence German workers.

The Communist Party was fractured. There was no central leadership, no newspaper or magazine, and no organization. However, Marx was not ready to let his beloved revolution die. During this period, Marx and Engels went undercover, posing as moderate democrats, hoping to spread their influence and secretly direct revolutionary policy away from mere democracy and toward communism. This repositioning made it possible for Marx to move among the more moderate groups without suspicion.

Comparing *Demands* and *Manifesto*

Demands of the Communist Party in Germany includes the right for all people ages 21 and older to vote; paid government representatives, so that workers could afford to hold office; universal arming of the people; free legal services; separation of church and state; and universal education. The document concludes with this appeal to the German people:

> It is to the interest of the German proletariat, the petty bourgeoisie and the small peasants to support these demands with all possible energy. Only by the realisation of these demands will the millions in Germany, who have hitherto been exploited by a handful of persons and whom the exploiters would like to keep in further subjection, win the rights and attain to that power to which they are entitled as the producers of all wealth.[1]

Demands of the Communist Party in Germany includes four of the ten points raised in the *Communist Manifesto* and proposes outright concessions to others. The four common points are graduated income tax, free education, state-owned transportation, and a national banking system.

Friedrich Wilhelm IV

ANOTHER NEWSPAPER AND MORE REVOLTS

By June 1848, Prussian king Friedrich Wilhelm
IV had been deposed, and Marx was free to return
to his homeland without fear of arrest. Once
there, Marx took over as editor of the *Neue Rheinische
Zeitung*. This newspaper, though backed by fellow

Communists from Brussels, appeared to support democratic ideals. But Marx had no intention of endorsing a democratic platform, and it was not long before his Communist agenda started to emerge in the paper's articles. He began attacking the leaders of the democratic movement.

In France, the proletarians were not happy. Representatives in the government abolished measures established earlier in the year to feed and provide for unemployed workers. Workers took to the streets in open revolt in what would come to be called the June Days Uprising. Marx praised the proletariat openly in the pages of the *Neue Rheinische Zeitung*. After the revolt was crushed, Marx openly lamented the thousands killed, trying to further justify the workers' cause. This open support of the French proletariat prompted the paper's backers and readers to pull away. Financing dwindled.

More Alienation by Marx

At a meeting of Cologne democrats in August 1848, Marx alienated his peers. A student who was present reported, "Everyone he treated with abject contempt; every argument that he did not like he answered either with biting scorn at the unfathomable ignorance that had prompted it. . . . It was very evident that not only had he not won any adherents, but had repelled many who otherwise might have become his followers."[2]

In Prussia, the middle-class delegates were trying to create a liberal constitution. Lower classes rioted in the streets, demanding more extreme social changes. Marx's followers were among the latter group. The revolt threatened middle-class interests. But King Friedrich Wilhelm IV retook control of the country with the support of the military. Ironically, the middle class, which had originally supported the revolution, now supported the king because of feeling threatened by the demands of Marx's followers. By September 1848, the revolution in Prussia was over.

Once the king retook the Prussian throne, he ordered the *Neue Rheinische Zeitung* shut down, but then changed his mind. The king realized it was better to keep radical ideas in the open where they could be monitored rather than having them disappear underground where they may fester, grow, and lead to more revolts.

Marx continued to use the paper to condemn the king's new government. Through its pages—and those of pamphlets—Marx urged rebellion, including armed resistance against the king's authority. In May 1849, the king eliminated the threat Marx posed by expelling him from the country, giving him

24 hours to leave, because he and Engels supported the insurgents against the Prussian government.

No Citizenship

While this was not the first instance of Marx being expelled from a country, this time was different. Since Marx had renounced his Prussian citizenship, he had no right to appeal his expulsion. He was now considered an alien in the country. He left Prussia behind and returned to Paris.

Marx was not welcomed to Paris the way he had been just after the revolution started. France had a new president, Louis-Napoléon. He did not welcome a revolutionary who might stir up trouble. Marx was not kicked out of the country, but he was restricted to the town of Morbihan, in northwest France. Marx lamented to Engels that the town was a malaria-infested marsh, and his placement

Engels Takes a Break from Revolution

As the revolutions of 1848 flared and then cooled, Engels seemed to lose his interest in the fight and withdrew. He traveled extensively in Europe, especially in France. His journal from this time is full of entries about the quality of the wine and the beauty of the women instead of the need for revolt. Engels tried to entice Marx to join him: "If there were no French-women, life wouldn't be worth living. But so long as there are [young Frenchwomen], well and good! That doesn't prevent one from some-times wishing to discuss a decent topic or enjoy life with a measure of refine-ment, neither of which is possible with anyone in the whole band of my acquaintances. You must come here."[3] The poverty-stricken Marx had no way to join his friend. After five weeks of wandering, Engels returned to Eng-land full of energy, ready again to take his place at Marx's side.

there was a veiled attempt by the French government to murder him and his family.

Marx appealed to other countries in Europe to give him residence, but most declined. The political upheaval in Europe was waning, and no country wanted a radical upstart in its midst. However, England had been virtually unscathed by the revolts in Europe, so the English government did not feel threatened by Marx's presence. In August 1849, Marx traveled to London, to live in exile.

Louis-Napoléon restricted Marx to Morbihan, France.

*Marx and his eldest daughter posed for a photograph in 1870.
Marx had a difficult time supporting his family.*

A HOME AT LAST

Once in London, Marx hoped to rise
in status and raise the proletariat with
him. He wanted to topple the British government
and erect proletarian rule in its place. Though the
revolutions of 1848 had failed and the owners of the

British factories thrived, Marx was undaunted. He was able to reason away the glitches in his writings that foretold the fall of bourgeois Europe.

FINANCIAL AND FAMILY TROUBLE

Marx's finances were dwindling, but he was able to secure a room to rent for his family through an acquaintance. There were seven in the Marx household: Marx and his wife, their four children, and a servant. Jenny was eight months pregnant when they settled in London. After some time, the family was able to rent a small apartment where Jenny gave birth to a boy. Both the boy and Jenny were sickly, and the family suffered in poverty.

In order to rekindle the fires of revolution, Marx began a newspaper to spread his ideas. Unfortunately, he had difficulty filling enough subscriptions to keep the paper in print. The revolutionaries whom

Delinquent Behavior

In addition to his revolutionary bent, Marx was also rowdy. During a night of heavy drinking in London, Marx and two friends entered a pub and proceeded to loudly insult all of the Englishmen there. They barely escaped the place and the patrons they had angered. By then, it was 2:00 a.m. As the three men stumbled home, one of the men shouted, "Hurrah, I have an idea!" and threw a stone, smashing the glass of a street lamp.[1] Marx and the other friend joined in. By the time it was over, the glass of five lamps lay in pieces on the street. The police heard the noise and chased them, but Marx and his friends escaped.

Marx's Character

Though Marx advocated absolute rule by the proletariat and equal rights for all, his leadership seemed quite the opposite. A Prussian spy who had personal contact with Marx wrote in a report, "The dominating trait of [Marx's] character is a limitless ambition and love of power. In spite of communist equality, which he keeps up his sleeve, he is the absolute ruler of his party. It is true that he does everything on his own, and he gives orders on his own responsibility and will endure no contradictions. All this, however concerns only his secret activity, and the secret sections. At public meetings of the party, he is on the contrary the most liberal and the most popular of them all."[2]

he had counted on to subscribe had substantially decreased in numbers. They had seen their revolutions fail and now, like Marx, were trying to feed themselves and their families. The paper closed after five issues. Marx faced failure again; this time, with even less money than before.

Soon, Marx and his family were evicted from their apartment. Their other creditors were alarmed, thinking the Marxes might flee, so they demanded full payment of outstanding bills. Having sold most everything they owned, the Marxes found themselves out on the street. Fortunately, they were able to save just enough money to pay for one week at a hotel.

Though their poverty continued to plague them, the Marxes were able to pay rent at the hotel for a few months. Jenny exhausted her resources; she begged from everyone she thought might help them. She was again pregnant when another terrible blow hit: the couple's one-year-old, who had been sick since birth, died. This was the beginning of some long, hard years for the Marx family.

MORE WORK FOR THE REVOLUTION

This was not a time of silence for Marx. Though his family suffered, he still maintained his ideals and believed revolution was imminent. He was under close watch by Prussian spies and the British. The Prussians gave an account of Marx's activities to the British ambassador to Berlin. The report said that Marx and others were planning the murder of Queen Victoria and other important Britons. The report continued that there were hundreds of groups in Germany alone, ready to begin the revolution. Though the numbers may have been exaggerated, it was true that Marx and Engels were planning the next revolt.

In 1850, the two wrote *A Plan of Action Against Democracy* and distributed it to the German members of the former League of the Just, which had been renamed the Communist League in June 1847. In this document, Marx instructed the revolutionaries to ally themselves with the bourgeoisie and gain their confidence. Once in place, the proletarians were to kill those in charge and then turn the revolution on the bourgeoisie and annihilate them.

Plan for a German Revolution

A Plan of Action Against Democracy aimed for a Communist takeover in Germany and laid out how the proletariat could take over the bourgeoisie. Marx believed this would have to be a bloody affair and instructed the proletariat to use whatever was at their disposal to depose the bourgeoisie, be it terrorism or open warfare. Apparently, after the proletarian victory, a Central Revolutionary Committee, with Marx and Engels as heads, would sweep in from outside Germany and take over.

The plan addresses this action to overthrow those in power, stating it is the society's aim:

The aim of the society is the overthrow of all the privileged classes, and to submit these classes to the dictatorship of the proletariat by maintaining the revolution in permanence until the realization of communism, which will be the last organizational form of the human family.[3]

Marx and Engels were proposing that the revolution continue until the bourgeoisie were eliminated, and the complete rule of the proletariat emerges as the last form of social and political system. While Marx held strongly to his beliefs, he never saw the dictates of the plan enacted.

Leading the Communist League became Marx's goal and Engels was ready to help. Marx and Engels began systematic attacks on anyone who disagreed with Marx's theories. Marx would attack his peers relentlessly, both on ideological and personal levels. Unfortunately, Marx needed the support of those he attacked in order to lead the league.

Starting *Das Kapital*

In the fall of 1850, Marx began one of his most influential works, *Das Kapital*. In it, he sought to examine capitalism objectively and scientifically, including its roots and its future. In doing so, he would examine profit, wage-labor, and production, among myriad other subjects.

Marx worked tirelessly for one full year on *Das Kapital*, but then he began to work on it less and less. Productive days would be followed by long periods of no writing at all. This on-again, off-again approach was typical of Marx.

From 1852 to 1862, Marx began his longest term of employment, writing articles for the *New York Daily Tribune*, a US newspaper. He averaged two articles per week. These consisted of Marx's opinions on current events in Europe. Engels wrote many of these articles, but allowed Marx to receive both credit and payment for them; it is not known how many articles Marx actually wrote. Although this was a steady job, the income covered only a small portion of Marx's living expenses.

In September 1864, Russian repression in Poland inspired workers from across Europe to assemble into what would become the International

Workingmen's Association, a
Communist organization. Marx was
invited to give the inaugural address
at the association's first conference.
In his speech, Marx focused on
reconciling differences and unifying
the group into a powerful European
body dedicated to spreading
communism. ⌒

International Workingmen's Association

Marx envisioned taking leadership of the International Workingmen's Association. Between 1864 and 1872, far from trying to unite the members, Marx and Engels followed what some called their normal course of divide and conquer. The two men attacked anyone they thought opposed them. Marx had some success in influencing the group's policy, but the organization was in decline by 1872.

Das Kapital.

Kritik der politischen Oekonomie.

Von

Karl Marx.

Erster Band.

Buch I: Der Produktionsprocess des Kapitals.

Das Recht der Uebersetzung wird vorbehalten.

Hamburg

Verlag von Otto Meissner.

1867.

New-York: L. W. Schmidt. 24 Barclay-Street.

In the fall of 1850, Marx started Das Kapital.

Marx in 1866

FINALLY COMPLETED

In 1866, Marx finally finished the first volume of *Das Kapital*. It had taken him 16 years to do so. Though he was known to be disorganized at times, a number of factors may have contributed to Marx's difficulty in finishing the work. In his correspondence with Engels from this time, Marx complained that he had become bored with the study of economics, the central element of *Das Kapital*. In addition, poverty and illness—his own and that suffered by family members—overshadowed these years. Marx also seemed more interested in attacking his competitors than finishing the book.

Das Kapital consists of four very long and complex books, the first of which was the only one to be published while Marx was alive. *Das Kapital* would become one of his best-known works, along with the *Communist Manifesto*. As with the *Communist Manifesto*, it would attract little attention during Marx's lifetime.

ECONOMIC THEORIES

In *Das Kapital*, Marx presented his ideas about how material goods get their value. He stated that the hours of physical labor it takes to make a product determine its value, and in this case, only physical labor should be considered labor. He called this labor-time. He considered this the only unit of value that should be considered when products are bought and sold. These were not new ideas. Adam Smith and David Ricardo, the fathers of the theory of modern capitalism, also believed in the labor theory of value.

The Imbalance of Capitalism

Marx believed there was an imbalance in the capitalist system. He stated in *Das Kapital*, "Accumulation of wealth at one pole is . . . at the same time accumulation of misery, the torment of [labor], slavery, ignorance, brutalization and moral degradation at the opposite pole."[1] Just like balancing a scale, Marx proposed that if wealth is distributed equally, society will be in balance, with no conflict between members of the society. But if one group accumulates the wealth, the other groups go without. The increased wealth of one group causes the increased poverty and suffering of the other groups, tipping the scales.

The amount of labor-time that goes into production determines the product's exchange-value, or worth in the marketplace. In Marx's system, a person should only need to work enough hours of labor-time to cover his or her daily needs. This is where Marx believed the capitalist system exploits the workers, because workers are forced to produce far more than they need.

The extra labor-time the proletarians work Marx called surplus value, which turns into capitalist profit. The workers do not benefit from the surplus. The bourgeoisie use the profits to buy more machinery and more land, on which they build factories. New factories mean more jobs, which results in more surplus value. Thus, the capitalist profits rise again. This sequence is repeated, with the bourgeoisie reaping more and more profit from the labor-time of the proletariat.

Marx also examined the impact of the Industrial Revolution and improving technology on the proletariat. As new machines become faster and more efficient, Marx asserted, they require fewer workers to run them. This leaves a portion of the proletariat unemployed. Since there are more workers to fill fewer jobs, the bourgeoisie are in a position to offer lower wages.

While this might seem good for capitalist profits, lower wages mean the proletariat can afford fewer goods. If fewer goods are sold, there is less profit and not as many workers are needed, so unemployment rises. The result is an economic depression.

During the depression, many

Marx's Poor Health

Marx suffered through a number of different ailments while writing *Das Kapital*. He could not sleep, his liver was ailing, and his stomach bothered him. He smoked nonstop and drank alcohol to excess. Although he suffered from boils all his life, Marx was particularly afflicted with them during the writing of *Das Kapital*. The boils would reach the size of a fist. The discomfort would distract him day and night. Marx wrote to his doctor:

Cut, lanced, etc., in short treated in every respect. . . . In spite of all this, the thing is continually breaking out again so that with the exception of two or three days I have been lying fallow for eight weeks. Last Saturday I went out again for the first time. On Monday came a relapse. I hope it will come to an end this week, but who will guarantee me against new eruptions? Moreover it sharply attacks my head.[2]

of the smaller capitalist enterprises are not able to survive on the lower profits. These businesses fail. The means of production fall into fewer capitalist hands. As the number of unemployed swells, the remaining capitalists make even more profits.

Marx was one of the first people to propose this theory of the business cycle in which prosperity leads to depression, recovery, and finally prosperity again. But Marx thought that as the cycle progressed, the depressions would worsen to the point that the proletariat would be so numerous and exploited that they would rise up and take over the factories. Then, the proletariat would, Marx assumed, create a world where workers would have all they needed.

DIFFICULT BUT RELEVANT

Das Kapital is not an easy read, and the way the book is organized makes it even more difficult to follow. Even Engels was not able to hold back some criticism of the final product:

> The train of thought is constantly interrupted by illustrations, and the point to be illustrated is never summarized after the illustration, so that one is forever plunging straight from the illustration of one point into

the exposition of another point. It is dreadfully tiring, and confusing, too.[3]

Moreover, many of the examples Marx used to substantiate his theories, such as the horrible exploitation of children as young as three working in the coal mines, were being addressed at the time in some respects. In capitalist Britain, workers and some capitalists were petitioning for better working conditions and affecting change. Marx tried to explain such reforms as part of his overall theory of revolution, since he saw them as results of working-class anger and government efforts to stem it. Marx actually took much of his information on the despicable working conditions from a government report meant to address those problems.

Even with its difficulty, some of Marx's ideas in *Das Kapital* have relevance today. For example, his

Relying on Others' Finances

Marx hoped *Das Kapital* would be successful enough to provide him with sufficient earnings so that he and his family could finally live comfortably and not rely on the support of others, namely his primary supporter, Engels. Marx wrote in a letter to Engels, "I hope and am firmly convinced that in the course of the next year I shall have acquired sufficient money to enable me to reform my economic situation from the ground up and at last stand once again on my own feet. Without you I would never have been able to bring my work to an end."[4]

theories of the business cycle are still useful. In many cases, however, where Marx predicted the proletariat would rise up due to exploitation, the proletariat has appealed to the government to assure improved working environments. Marx did not foresee the intervention of the government with reforms that protected the workers. Instead of the pure capitalist system against which Marx raged, many economies became a mixture of capitalist and socialist policies. ⌒

A Thank You to Engels

After completing the final revisions of volume one of *Das Kapital*, Marx sent a thank you note to Engels. He wrote, "So, this volume is finished. I owe it to you alone that it was possible! Without your self-sacrifice for me I could not possibly have managed the immense [labor] demanded by the three volumes. I embrace you, full of thanks."[5]

Engels helped Marx write Das Kapital.

Das Kapital *did not sell as well as Marx had hoped.*

FINAL YEARS

fter years of abject poverty, Marx spent his final years in relative material comfort. In 1868, the ever-loyal Engels sold his share of his family's textile firm and set up an annual stipend for Marx of 350 pounds, or $574—a substantial sum in those days. Marx was also willed a large sum by a follower. He earned little income through work the last ten years of his life. He was certain *Das Kapital* would bring him attention and financial success, but the publication was not well received. Marx was paid 60 pounds, or $88.41, for the first printing of 1,000 books, which took four years to sell.

In his typical fashion, Marx did not blame the poor sales on the book's lack of organization or its erratic focus. Instead, he blasted economists for their negative critiques, deeming those who reviewed the book poorly, enemies claiming they were trying to sabotage his success.

ACTIVIST AGAIN

Once *Das Kapital* was complete in 1866, Marx did not write much more. He traded his pen once again

Messy Handwriting

After Marx's death, Engels began editing the second and third volume of *Das Kapital* and organizing and translating Marx's unpublished works. This was a difficult task for many reasons. There were thousands of pages, and the work was disorganized. One of the greatest obstacles to translating the work was Marx's handwriting, which, as one biographer stated, "resembled strings of barbed wire waving in the wind."[1]

for the banner of the activist. He was very involved in the International Workingmen's Association, holding the position of secretary in the German group. He also held sway in the powerful local London unit of the association.

As the International Workingmen's Association grew, Marx had more difficulty imposing his policies. The number of groups in Europe was increasing, and they banded together by nationality instead of being defined by the common cause of the proletariat. The headquarters of the International Workingmen's Association was moved to the United States. This marked the beginning of the end for the organization.

From the late 1860s to the early 1870s, wars broke out in Europe, and Marx's hopes rose with each one. As the wars flared, he waited in anticipation for the proletarian

A Kind and Funny Father

After Marx's death, his surviving daughter, Eleanor, addressed the gentle and brutal aspects of her father's personality. "To those students of human nature, it will not seem strange that this man, who was such a fighter, should at the same time be the kindliest and gentlest of men. They will understand that he could hate so fiercely only because he could love so profoundly . . . that if his sarcastic [humor] could bite like a corrosive acid, that same [humor] could be as balm to those in trouble and afflicted."[2]

revolution to break out. Writing hundreds of letters to people across Europe requesting support for rebels, Marx flung himself into the cause. To his disappointment, every group Marx backed was either defeated or deposed. Seeing the rise of the proletariat during his lifetime became a dwindling hope.

Personal Life Changes

While Marx had material comfort during this time, other personal matters weighed on him. His family was shrinking. As each of his three daughters married and moved out, the Marx household became smaller. Marx was a doting father, and he missed his girls. In addition, the men his daughters married had no sense of responsibility. Marx ached for his daughters when he heard about their unhappy marriages.

Another painful matter was that his wife, Jenny, was diagnosed with cancer. As she suffered, Marx's health plummeted as well. The boils which plagued him during the writing of *Das Kapital* returned with a vengeance. He also endured neuralgia, a painful condition of the nerves, and liver problems. Unable to rest due to insomnia and anxiety over his daughters' situations, Jenny's health, and his own physical ailments, Marx lived in a wretched state. In 1881, Jenny died.

Marx, having contracted pneumonia and pleurisy, both of which made his breathing painful, tried to move to a place with a healthier climate. He had the money to travel and wandered from Algeria to France to Switzerland seeking the fine weather these places usually promised. Unfortunately, his quest was unsuccessful; every place he went, clouds covered the

Marx's Eulogy

As Engels stood at Marx's graveside, he began to eulogize his longtime friend with these words:

On March 14, at a quarter to three in the afternoon, the greatest living thinker ceased to think. For scarcely two minutes he had been left alone, and when we came back we found him in his easy chair peacefully sleeping—but forever.

No one can measure the loss that has been sustained by the aggressive proletariat of Europe and America, and by historical science, in the death of this man. Soon enough men will come to feel the void which the death of this powerful spirit has torn into the fabric of things.[3]

Engels went on to say that Marx was a man without enemies, and that, when attacked, he would brush aside any abuse "as though they were spiders' webs, paying no attention to them."[4] Given Marx's quick temper toward those he felt opposed him, it was an interesting statement. Engels also characterized Marx as a refugee, deported by the governments of Europe. But it is also true that in his later life, Marx was able to travel freely in France and Germany, two countries he had hoped would erupt in revolution, and he was never at risk of deportation by England.

sun, and the skies poured down rain. While traveling, Marx heard the news of his daughter's death and rushed back to London. Shortly thereafter, he was diagnosed with an abscess of the lungs, a dangerous bacterial infection. Coughing up pus and in misery, Marx was ordered to bed.

On the afternoon of Wednesday, March 14, 1883, Engels arrived for his daily visit with Marx. During the visit, Engels left Marx's side for a few minutes. When he returned, Marx was dead. The funeral was set for the following Saturday. Engels wrote many letters to alert those in the International Workingmen's Association and other workers' groups, thinking that many of them would come to pay their last respects to the man who ferociously championed their cause. But Marx was buried with little fanfare. Although he had spoken out for leagues of workers time and again

Marx's Epitaph

Marx's original grave in London's Highgate Cemetery was simple and obscure, and he shared it with the rest of his family. Eventually, the British Communist Party had his remains moved to a prominent part of the cemetery, and crowned it with a large headstone made of marble and bronze. The epitaph is from Marx's own writing: "Philosophers have only interpreted the world in various ways. The point is to change it."[5]

regardless of the danger, his funeral party was meager; only a small group of friends and relatives were present.

Engels read the eulogy to those assembled, predicting of Marx, "His name and his work will live for centuries to come."[6] But not even Engels, who held Marx's theories in such high esteem, could predict the tremendous impact his friend's ideas would have on the twentieth century and beyond.

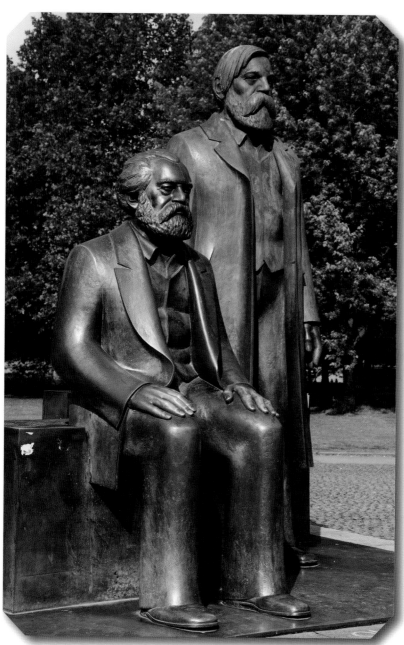

Statues of Marx and Engels in Germany

Vladimir Ilyich Lenin

MARX AND MARXISM

While Marx was alive, his written works were little more than ignored. Only a generation later, they were used to generate a tidal wave of revolution. In November 1917, Vladimir Ilyich Lenin led the proletariat of Russia in revolt against Czar Nicholas II. Lenin rose to power. For the rest of the twentieth century, his take on Marxist theory would be adapted and adopted by one-third of the world's population. Although Marx preached revolution of the workers, and Lenin's Marxism did lead to many improvements for workers, the system he created, especially when it was later used by Joseph Stalin, would also be used to assert tight and often terrifying control over the proletariat.

Marx did not leave much detail about how to construct the egalitarian world the proletariat ruled. His works were mostly concerned with the evils of capitalism and how to bring about capitalism's total destruction. Marx thought such a blueprint was impossible, since history could only be made by the people actually living it rather than by intellectual theorists. When Marx's devotees united to follow Lenin during the Russian Revolution, Lenin created his own version of Marxism. In essence, the political methods of Russia and the

"The Marxist doctrine is omnipotent because it is true. It is comprehensive and harmonious, and provides men with an integral world outlook irreconcilable with any form of superstition, reaction, or defense of bourgeois oppression. It is the legitimate successor to the best that man produced in the nineteenth century, as represented by German philosophy, English political economy and French socialism."[1]

—*Vladimir Lenin,*
On Culture and
Cultural Revolution

other Communist countries that emerged in the twentieth century did not accurately reflect Marx's ideas.

Marxism, Leninism, Stalinism

Following the Russian Revolution of 1917, after which Russia became the Soviet Union, the Communist leadership enacted some of Marx's theories. Among other changes, inheritance was revoked and private property was abolished. But since Marx had left no blueprint for a purely Communist society, Lenin and his contemporaries had to produce solutions that sometimes contradicted Marx's own values. For example, in order to feed the Russian army, Lenin enacted a policy that paid the farmers far less than what their crops were worth, essentially devaluing their labor-time.

One of the early changes Lenin instituted was that the proletariat should not be allowed to lead the revolution, as Marx had proposed, but that the revolution should be led by an elite group of politically committed Communists from the educated middle-class, of which Marx and Lenin are examples. Another difference is that Marx theorized

Joseph Stalin

that revolution would spring from an industrialized society that had a large proletariat, while Lenin proposed that the proletariat had been influenced so much by capitalism that its members were unable to lead a true revolution. Lenin asserted

that revolution could also come in an agricultural
society like Russia. Other changes were to follow that
would stray from Marxist theory, so much so that
the guiding principles of the Soviet Union could no
longer accurately be called Marxism—they were called
Marxism-Leninism.

Joseph Stalin followed Lenin as the leader of the
Communist Party in the Soviet Union in 1924 after
Lenin's death. While Lenin believed the proletariat
needed the guidance of an educated elite, Stalin
believed the Communist Party needed to be guided
by a single leader, namely himself. Other policies
would follow that would lead the Communist Soviet
Union away from Marx's theory—especially rule by
political dictatorship backed heavily by force. But to
the citizens of the world, the name of Marx would be
closely associated with the Soviet Union's system of
government.

After Stalin's death in 1953, the Soviet system
moved more toward rule by bureaucracy and the
country was powerful enough to challenge the
United States as a world superpower in the Cold
War. But by the 1980s, the once powerful Soviet
Union was wracked by inefficiency and debt. Soviet
President Mikhail Gorbachev tried to reform his

nation to move it in democratic and capitalistic directions. But it was too late. In 1991, the republics that made up the Soviet Union asserted their independence. Soviet communism and the Soviet Union dissolved.

COMMUNISM AROUND THE WORLD

In 1949, another revolutionary movement claimed Marxist theory as its backbone. Communist revolutionary Mao Zedong eventually led the revolt in the People's Republic of China that started in the 1920s and triumphed in 1949. Just as Lenin and Stalin before him, Mao's version of Marxist thought became known by another name—Mao Zedong Thought. Like Lenin, Mao claimed that, contrary to Marx, the Communist revolution could come from an unindustrialized, agricultural China. Mao proposed that China was a proletarian country that was victimized by other

Denouncing Stalin's Tactics

Stalin violated the spirit of Marxism and even Leninism by installing himself as omnipotent leader of the Soviet Union. In the twenty-first century, Soviet Premier Nikita Khrushchev denounced Stalin's violation of Marxism-Leninism, saying, "It is impermissible and foreign to the spirit of Marxism-Leninism to elevate one person, to transform him into a superman possessing supernatural characteristics akin to those of a god."[2]

capitalist countries, similar to how the proletariat was victimized by capitalists. Similar to Stalin in the Soviet Union, Mao became the supreme power in China, though he relied less on top-down force than on mobilizing the masses to reach revolutionary goals.

Similar cases have happened in other parts of the world, such as Cuba and North Korea, with the same result: rule by an undemocratic Communist Party rather than the proletariat. But in all cases, no matter how far from Marx's original theories they strayed, these countries consider Marx the father of their political thought.

In addition to affecting the histories of some countries, Marx also had a great effect on those who used his name to define what they were not. In the twentieth century, nations in the Western political world defined themselves in terms of their

"Revolution is not a dinner party, nor an essay, nor a painting, nor a piece of embroidery; it cannot be advanced softly, gradually, carefully, considerately, respectfully, politely, plainly, and modestly. A revolution is an insurrection, an act of violence by which one class overthrows another."[3]

—Mao Zedong

differences from the Communist Soviet Union and the rest of the Communist world.

The seeds that Marx planted in the course of history—his ideas about the value of labor, the purity of the proletariat, the villainy of capitalism, and the progress of history itself—sprouted, developed, and changed the landscape of the world in ways that are still being discovered. Marx was an egotistical, brilliant, and passionate man who fought for his beliefs, even if he had to attack others

The Soviet Union Offers Guidance

After Mao climbed to power in 1949, he looked to his Communist comrades to the north for assistance. He turned to Stalin for ideological and material help. Stalin, although suspecting Mao's dedication to communism, was not convinced of China's worth as an ally until China took up arms to aid Communist North Korea in the Korean War. Stalin also did not like the idea of a large rival to Soviet leadership of the Communist world.

Mao admitted to copying Stalin's methods when it came to policy. Mao and his leadership were skilled at guerilla warfare and inciting the peasantry to riot, but they had no experience running an industrialized nation. The Soviets assisted the Chinese in drawing up a workable plan for the future. The Soviets remained as technical advisers and provided aid in developing Chinese factories. By the late 1950s, however, Soviet-Chinese relations began to unravel.

Cuba offered a similar story. In 1959, Communist forces led by Fidel Castro took control of the Cuban government and created a Communist regime. Shortly thereafter, Castro negotiated a trade agreement with the Soviets. Over the next 30 years, the Soviet Union would be Cuba's largest trading partner. In addition to providing goods, the Soviets also provided Cuba with weapons and subsidies.

to do so. He imagined himself the leader of the true political path that he developed. In some eyes, he was a scourge; in others, a saint. But it cannot be denied that, just as Engels had predicted while standing at Marx's graveside, Marx has greatly influenced the course of history.

Marx's grave in London

TIMELINE

1818	1824	1830
Karl Heinrich Marx is born in Trier, Prussia, on May 5.	Though Jewish, Marx is baptized Lutheran because of anti-Semitism.	Marx enters grade school at Trier Gymnasium in October.

1842	1843	1844
Marx moves to Cologne, Prussia, to edit the *Rheinische Zeitung*.	Marx marries Jenny von Westphalen. They move to Paris, France.	Marx begins a lifelong relationship with Friedrich Engels.

1835–1836

Marx attends the University of Bonn.

1836

Marx begins attending the University of Berlin.

1841

Marx receives his doctorate.

1845

Marx moves to Brussels, Belgium, and founds the Communist Party.

1847

Marx joins the League of the Just, which is soon renamed the Communist League.

1848

The *Communist Manifesto* is first printed in February.

TIMELINE

1848

Marx is expelled from Brussels, and he writes *Demands of the Communist Party in Germany.*

1848

In June, Marx returns to Cologne, Prussia, to edit the *Neue Rheinische Zeitung.*

1849

Marx is expelled from Prussia and returns to Paris, France. King Louis-Napoléon sends Marx to live in the north.

1864

The International Workingmen's Association is formed. Marx gives the inaugural address at the association's first conference.

1866

Marx completes *Das Kapital, Volume One.*

Das Kapital.

Kritik der politischen Oekonomie.

Karl Marx.

1849	1850	1852
Marx moves to London, England, in August.	Marx and Engels write *A Plan of Action Against Democracy.*	Marx begins to write for the *New York Daily Tribune.*

1883		1917
Marx dies in London, England, on March 14.		Inspired by Marx, Vladimir Lenin leads the Russian Revolution.

Essential Facts

Date of Birth

May 5, 1818

Place of Birth

Trier, Prussia (modern-day Germany)

Date of Death

March 14, 1883

Parents

Heinrich and Henriette Marx

Education

University of Bonn, University of Berlin

Marriage

Jenny von Westphalen (June 19, 1843)

Children

Jenny Caroline, Jenny Laura, Edgar, Henry Edward Guy, Jenny Eveline Frances, Jenny Julia Eleanor

Career Highlights

Marx found a friend in Friedrich Engels. The two worked together on many publications. Marx's work helped ignite several uprisings and revolutions against the bourgeoisie in Europe during the mid-1800s.

Societal Contribution

Many of Marx's publications changed the way governments today operate. Marx's work inspired workers and citizens to rise up against those that oppressed them. However, these revolutionary attempts often resulted in violence, which Marx encouraged.

Conflicts

Throughout his career, Marx made enemies with many European governments, most notably Belgium, France, and Prussia. He also alienated some people who may have been interested in his cause by harshly critiquing their work and ideas. In March 1848, Marx and his wife, Jenny, were arrested in Brussels, Belgium. They were freed and ordered to leave the country.

Quote

"Communists scorn to hide their views and aims. They openly declare that their purposes can only be achieved by the forcible overthrow of the entire existing social order. Let the ruling classes tremble at a Communist revolution. The proletarians have nothing to lose but their chains. They have a world to win. Workingmen of all countries, unite!" —*Karl Marx,* Communist Manifesto

GLOSSARY

aristocracy
> The highest social class; also a government run by that class.

atheism
> Belief that there is no God.

benefactor
> A person who helps someone through effort, financial, or material support.

bourgeoisie
> According to Karl Marx, the people in a capitalist system who own the factories and property and profit from the labor of the workers.

business cycle
> A cycle of production and consumption that moves from prosperity to depression to recovery, then repeats.

capitalism
> A system in which all industry is privately owned and regulated and profits go to the owners rather than the producers or the state.

communism
> A system in which the proletariat rises to power by eliminating capitalism completely, all private property is abolished, and workers work according to their ability and are paid according to their needs.

dialectic
> The process by which the result of two conflicting ideas produces an altogether new idea; in Hegelian terms thesis + antithesis = synthesis.

editor
> The person responsible for determining the content of a text, such as a newspaper or magazine.

egalitarian
> The principle that all people are equal and deserve equal opportunities.

exile
> A person kept from entering or living in his or her home country.

feudalism
> A social system in which lords were bound in service to a king in exchange for land; peasants worked the land and provided the lords with a percentage of their labor or products. In this system, there was no movement among social classes.

incarceration
> Being arrested and held in jail.

insurrection
> A rebellion against rulers or government, often involving armed conflict.

manifesto
> A declaration of policy.

philosopher
> A person who examines the nature of existence.

philosophy
> Study of the basic underlying principles of a subject.

proletariat
> In Marxist terms, the workers in a capitalist system, who are paid by the hour; as capitalist profits rise the proletariat work longer hours for lower wages.

reform
> To change gradually and peacefully for the better.

socialism
> A system in which the entire community plays a part in owning, producing, and sharing products, services, and government.

ADDITIONAL RESOURCES

SELECTED BIBLIOGRAPHY

Blumenberg, Werner. *Portrait of Marx*. New York: Herder and Herder, 1972. Print.

Liebknecht, Wilhelm. *Karl Marx: Biographical Memoirs*. New York: Greenwood, 1968. Print.

McLellan, David. *Karl Marx: A Biography*. New York: Palgrave Macmillan, 2006. Print.

Rius. *Marx for Beginners*. New York: Pantheon, 1976. Print.

FURTHER READINGS

Strathern, Paul. *Marx in 90 Minutes*. Chicago: Ivan R. Dee, 2001. Print.

Vander Hook, Sue. *Communism*. Edina, MN: Abdo, 2011. Print.

Wheen, Francis. *Karl Marx: A Life*. New York: Norton, 2001. Print.

Web Links

To learn more about Karl Marx, visit ABDO Publishing Company online at **www.abdopublishing.com**. Web sites about Karl Marx are featured on our Book Links page. These links are routinely monitored and updated to provide the most current information available.

Places to Visit

Highgate Cemetery
Swain's Lane, London, Highgate, N6 6PJ, United Kingdom
(44) 020-8340-1834
http://www.highgate-cemetery.org
Marx is buried in the cemetery. A huge headstone and bust of Marx crown his grave.

Marx's Childhood Home
Brückenstrasse 10, 54290 Trier, Germany
http://www.fes.de/marx/index_e.htm
Marx's childhood home is now a museum commemorating his life and work.

Source Notes

Chapter 1. Insurrection and Arrest

1. Alexis de Tocqueville. *Recollections: The French Revolution of 1848*. New York: Doubleday, 1970. Print. 98.

2. Francis Wheen. *Karl Marx: A Life*. New York: Norton, 2001. Print. 118.

Chapter 2. Childhood and School Days

1. Robert Payne. *Marx*. New York: Simon & Schuster, 1968. Print. 345.

2. Craig, Edward, ed. *Routledge Encyclopedia of Philosophy: Volume 6*. New York: Routledge, 1998. Print. 121.

Chapter 3. A Journalist

1. Francis Wheen. *Karl Marx: A Life*. New York: Norton, 2001. Print. 36–37.

2. Ibid. 43.

3. Ibid. 48.

Chapter 4. Committing to Communism

1. Francis Wheen. *Karl Marx: A Life*. New York: Norton, 2001. Print. 80.

2. Ibid. 169.

3. Ibid.

4. Ibid. 42.

5. Ibid.

6. Ibid. 169.

7. Ibid.

8. Hannah Arendt. *Between Past and Future*. New York: Penguin Classics, 1993. Print. 21.

Chapter 5. A Famous Text

1. Francis Wheen. *Karl Marx: A Life*. New York: Norton, 2001. Print. 117.

2. Ibid.

3. Ibid. 115.

4. Albert Alexander. *Karl Marx: Father of Modern Socialism*. New York: Franklin Watts, 1969. Print. 62.

5. Robert Payne. *Marx*. New York: Simon & Schuster, 1968. Print. 174.

6. Ibid. 173.

Chapter 6. Editor Again

1. "Demands of the Communist Party in Germany." *Marxists Internet Archive*. Marxists Internet Archive Admin Committee, n.d. Web. 10 Jan. 2011.

2. Ibid.

3. Robert Payne. *Marx*. New York: Simon & Schuster, 1968. Print. 129.

Chapter 7. A Home at Last

1. Robert Payne. *Marx*. New York: Simon & Schuster, 1968. Print. 282.

2. Ibid. 254.

3. Ibid. 241.

Source Notes Continued

Chapter 8. Finally Completed

1. Francis Wheen. *Karl Marx: A Life*. New York: Norton, 2001. Print. 301.

2. Robert Payne. *Marx*. New York: Simon & Schuster, 1968. Print. 348.

3. Francis Wheen. *Karl Marx: A Life*. New York: Norton, 2001. Print. 312.

4. Robert Payne. *Marx*. New York: Simon & Schuster, 1968. Print. 395.

5. Francis Wheen. *Karl Marx: A Life*. New York: Norton, 2001. Print. 298.

Chapter 9. Final Years

1. Francis Wheen. *Karl Marx: A Life*. New York: Norton, 2001. Print. 125.

2. David McLellan. *Karl Marx: A Biography*. New York: Palgrave Macmillan, 2006. Print. 429.

3. Robert Payne. *Marx*. New York: Simon & Schuster, 1968. Print. 500.

4. Ibid. 502.

5. Barry Smart. *Michel Foucault: Critical Assessments*. London: Routledge, 1994. Print. 322.

6. Robert Payne. *Marx*. New York: Simon & Schuster, 1968. Print. 511.

Chapter 10. Marx and Marxism
    1. V. I. Lenin. *On Culture and Cultural Revolution*. Rockville, MD: Wildside, 2008. Print. 35.
    2. Trisha Ziff. *Che Guevara: Revolutionary & Icon*. New York: Abrams Image, 2006. Print. 66.
    3. William Safire. *Lend Me Your Ears: Great Speeches in History*. New York: Norton, 2004. Print. 965.

INDEX

ABOUT THE AUTHOR

David Cates is an author and teacher. He has written and taught English in diverse locations around the world, including India, Nepal, and Japan. Cates lives in Georgia with his family.

PHOTO CREDITS